COMMON WILDFLOWERS OF WESTERN AUSTRALIA

Introduction

In Western Australia, botanists to date have identified over 10,000 vascular plants. It is understandable that a visitor to this vast huge State would find the quantity and variation of wildflowers simply overwhelming. This small publication attempts to illustrate some of the more easily identifiable common and not so common wildflowers.

Rather than confuse the traveller with the differing vegetation zones, the wildflower illustrations have been divided into those plants that can be seen in the Perth region, those north of Perth and finally those that can be seen when travelling South and east of Perth.

Under each photograph the plants common and Latin name will appear. There is also a blank area to write in where and when you may have seen that particular specie.

It is interesting to note that in the South West Province alone, 80% of the plant specie can only be found in that region and that overall, 62% of the total plant specie can only be found in Western Australia, testimony to the unique richness of this State.

We hope you enjoy your journey in one of the richest flora regions of the World.

WESTERN AUSTRALIA'S

The map on this page shows the 3 major botanic zones in Western Australia. The Northern Province. The Eremaean Province and the South-West Province.

Within these regions can be found many varying types of habitat from heathlands, tall forests, open acacia woodland etc but for general interest we have overlaid (schematically) the varying densities of wildflower specie that may found in each region. This may help you identify the richest areas when travelling. There are however some particular areas that have amazing high densities of flora (we call these, flora specie hot spots) such as localities like Mount Lesueur, Eneabba sandplain, Kalbarri National Park, Fitzgerald National Park, The Ravensthorpe Range. Stirling Range National Park, Tarrin Rock Nature Reserve, Harrismith Nature Reserve to name but a few. No one region however is lacking in large numbers of plants so even the lowest density regions of specie diversification is still classed as moderate.

Areas like the Kimberley, the Pilbara, and the Shark Bay Region contain a huge wealth of plant life. Even the deserts after rain show a wealth of plant life that has remained dormant until the first winter or cyclonic rains.

■ Extremely High ■ Very High ■ High ■ Moderately High
■ Moderate

Geographic Regions

1. Perth Environs
2. South West
3. South Coast
4. Wheatbelt
5. Goldfields & Transitional Woodland
6. Nullarbor
7. Mid West
8. Mulga
9. Shark Bay Region & North West Coast
10. Pilbara
11. Deserts
12. Kimberley

AJOR BOTANIC REGIONS

12
WYNDHAM

NORTHERN PROVINCE
(Kimberley Region)

BROOME

PORT HEDLAND

Tanami Desert

Great Sandy Desert

11

9

10

CARNARVON

EREMAEAN PROVINCE
(Pilbara & Desert Region)

Little Sandy Desert

Gibson Desert

8

Victoria Desert

7

5

6

KALGOORLIE

SOUTH-WEST PROVINCE

PERTH

1

4

2

3

ESPERANCE

ALBANY

3

12

11

10

7

8

9

WILDFLOWERS OF THE PERTH REGION

Grasstree
Xanthorrhoea preissii

Where............................ Date.................

Wilsons Grevillea
Grevillea wilsonii

Where............................ Date.................

Purple Flags
Patersonia occidentalis

Where............................. Date.............

Red and Green Kangaroo Paw
Anigozanthos manglessii

Where............................ Date.................

Marri
Corymbia calaphylla

Where............................ Date.................

The Darling Range runs parallel to the coast over 200km. The Darling scarp shown above contains some of the richest flora areas in the Perth region. Plants like Candle Cranberry. Grace

Drumstick Isopogon
Isopogon sphaerocephalus

Where............................ Date.................

Bull Banksia
Banksia grandis

Where............................ Date.................

Pindak
Calothamnus sanguineus

Where............................ Date.............

Many-flowered Honeysuckle
Lambertia multiflora subsp darlingensis

Where.......................... Date.................

Candle Cranberry
Astroloma foliosum

Where.......................... Date.................

Honeymyrtle, Plumed Featherflower Many-flowered Honeysuckle and Fuchsia Grevillea grow here in profusion in the spring.

Plummed Featherflower
Verticordia plumosa

Where.......................... Date.................

Graceful Honeymyrtle
Melaleuca radula

Where.......................... Date.................

Fuchsia Grevillea
Grevillea bipinnatifida

Where.......................... Date.................

Rough Honeymyrtle
Melaleuca parviceps

Where.......................... Date.................

Menzies Banksia
Banksia menziesii

Where.......................... Date.................

Milkwort
Comesperma confertum

Where.......................... Date.................

WILDFLOWERS OF THE PERTH REGION

Bacon and Eggs
Oxylobium capitatum

Where........................... Date.................

Red Lechenaultia
Lechenaultia formosa

Where........................... Date.................

Hooded Lily
Johnsonia lupulina

Where........................... Date.............

Pink Summer Calytrix
Calytrix fraseri

Where........................... Date.................

Prickly Bitterpea
Daviesia decurrens

Where........................... Date.................

In the open Wandoo Woodland *(Eucalyptus wa doo)* many of our stunning orchids can be foun such as Blood Spider, Splendid White Spider ar Blue China Orchid all shown opposite. A couple th author knows has found over 36 specie of orch under Wandoo and acacia woodland alongside ju

Prickly Moses
Acacia pulchella

Where........................... Date.................

Devils Pins
Hovea pungens

Where........................... Date.................

Swan River Myrtle
Hypocalymma robustum

Where........................... Date............

Crimson Spider Orchid
Caladenia footteiana

Where............................. Date.................

Slendid White Spider Orchid
Caladenia splendens

Where............................. Date.................

Blue China Orchid
Cyanicula gemmata

Where............................. Date.................

ne small creek in Wandoo Conservation Park.
Within the pea family *(Fabaceae)* there are many
enera and literally hundreds of specie in Australia.
wo are depicted here on left page. Bacon and
ggs, Prickly Bitter pea and Devils Pins all belong
o different genera.

White Myrtle
Hypocalymma angustifolium

Where............................. Date.................

Scented Banjine
Pimelea suaveolens

Where............................. Date.................

hristmas Tree
uytsia floribunda

here........................... Date.................

Pom Poms
Ptilotus manglesii

Where........................... Date.................

Hairy Jugflower
Adenanthos barbigerus

Where........................... Date.................

WILDFLOWERS SOUTH OF PERTH

Drumsticks
Kingia australis

Where........................... Date................

Opossum's-tails
Anersonia caerulea

Where........................... Date................

Red Ink Sundew
Drosera erythrorhiza

Where........................... Date..............

Bird Orchid
Pterostylis barbata

Where........................... Date................

Saltwater Paperbark
Melaleuca cuticularis

Where........................... Date................

The deep southwest is home to the tall Kar (*Eucalyptus diversicolor*) forest. Under the towering trees in late spring the beautiful purple colour of the Tree Hovea contrasts with the bright yellow flowers

Coastal Foxglove
Ptyrodia exserta

Where........................... Date................

A Beaufortia
Beaufortia incana

Where........................... Date................

Basket Flower
Adenanthos obovatus

Where........................... Date................

arri Hazel
ymaliun spathulatum

Where......................... Date.................

White Banjine
Pimelea ciliata

Where......................... Date.................

Tassel Flower
Leucopogon verticillatus

Where......................... Date.................

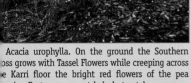

Acacia urophylla. On the ground the Southern
oss grows with Tassel Flowers while creeping across
e Karri floor the bright red flowers of the pea
unning Postman can not help but catch ones eye.

An Acacia
Acacia urophylla

Where......................... Date.................

Swamp Daisy
Actinodium cunninghamii

Where......................... Date.................

ee Hovea
ovea elliptica

here......................... Date.................

Running Postman
Kennedia prostrata

Where......................... Date.................

Southern Cross
Xanthosia rotundifolia

Where......................... Date.................

WILDFLOWERS SOUTH OF PERTH

Albany Bottlebrush
Callistemon speciosa

Where.......................... Date...............

Handsome Wedge Pea
Gompholobium venustum

Where.......................... Date...............

Swamp Bottlebrush
Beaufortia sparsa

Where.......................... Date...............

Yellow Trumpets
Conostylis bealiana

Where....................... Date...............

Mount Barren Grevillea
Grevillea macrostylis

Where.......................... Date...............

As one drives along the southern coast the speci
density of flora slowly increases. The bright vermilio
flowers of the Swamp Bottlebrush are seen along th
South West Highway in the winter wet areas in lat
spring early summer. Also closer to Albany the aptl
named Albany Bottlebrush becomes numerous.
If the traveller has time to venture on to th

Round leaved Pigface
Disphyma crassifolium

Where.......................... Date...............

Red Rod
Eremophila calorhabdos

Where.......................... Date...............

Sticky tailflower
Anthoceris viscosa

Where.......................... Date...............

Qualup Bell
Pimelea physodes, red flowered form

Where........................... Date.................

Royal Hakea
Hakea victoria

Where........................... Date.................

Hakea pandanicarpa

Where........................... Date.................

Fitzgerald River National Park one is treated to maybe the greatest selection of wildflowers the southwest has to offer with over 1800 specie. Here the Qualup Bell and The stunning Royal Hakea above adorn the side of the dirt tracks. The above photo shows the coastline at East Mt Barren with rare wildflowers in the foreground. *(Please see note at rear of booklet.)*

Oak-leaved Dryandra
Dryandra quercifolia

Where........................... Date.................

Cauliflower Hakea
Hakea corymbosa

Where........................... Date.................

Woody Pear
Xylomelum angustifolium

Where........................... Date.................

Sea Urchin Hakea
Hakea petiolaris

Where........................... Date.................

Hood-leaved Hakea
Hakea cucullata

Where........................... Date.................

Gardners Banksia
Banksia gardneri subsp. gardneri

Where.......................... Date................

Creeping banksia
Banksia repens

Where.......................... Date................

Scarlet Banksia
Banksia coccinea

Where.......................... Date................

Nodding Banksia
Banksia nutans subsp. cernuella

Where.......................... Date................

Caleys Banksia
Banksia Caleyi

Where.......................... Date................

All along the southern coast one can see man
Banksias growing. Above is the view looking to Bo
Island and here the Cutleaf Banksia *(Banksia pra*
morsa) grows. As one journeys through th
Fitzgerald River National Park many Banksias can b
found including Baxter's Banksia. Nodding Banksi

Baxters Banksia
Banksia baxteri

Where.......................... Date................

Red Swamp banksia
Banksia occidentalis subsp. occidentalis

Where.......................... Date................

Showy banksia
Banksia speciosa

Where.......................... Date................

allerak
ucalyptus pleurocarpa

Vhere............................ Date.................

Red-flowering Gum
Corymbia ficifolia

Where............................ Date.................

Cut-leaf Hibbertia
Hbbertia cuneiformis

Where............................ Date.................

anksia gardeneri var. hiemalis and Caley's Banksia.
he coastline around Esperance is breath taking and
ast is the National parks of Cape Le Grande and
ape Arid also have a wealth of wildflowers. The
illsides can be covered with a thick over storey of
nowy Banksia.

Vanilla Orchid
Thelymitra antennifera

Where............................ Date.................

Curry Flower
Lysinema cilatum

Where............................ Date.................

horilaena
horilaena quercifolia

Vhere............................ Date.................

Woodbridge Poison
Isotoma hypocrateriformis

Where............................ Date.................

Cowslip Orchid
Caladenia flava subsp. flava

Where............................ Date.................

WILDFLOWERS SOUTH OF PERTH

Compass Bush
Allocasuarina pinaster

Where......................... Date.................

Heath-leaved Honeysuckle
Lambertia ericifolia

Where......................... Date.................

Cork Bark Honeymyrtle
Melaleuca suberosa

Where......................... Date.................

Baxters Kunzea
Kunzea baxteri

Where......................... Date.................

Long-leaved Cone Bush
Petophile longifolia

Where......................... Date.................

One area that is not only beautiful with its mountain backdrop but is noted for its vast selection of wildflowers is the Stirling Range. Here many plants only grow here. Many like some of the 'bells', grow high up on the mountain slopes. Here two of the

Broad-leaved Poison
Brachysema latifolium

Where......................... Date.................

Green Botlebrush
Melaleuca diosmifolia

Where......................... Date.................

Shirt Orchid
Thelymitra campanulata

Where......................... Date.................

tirling Range Coneflower
Isopogon baxteri

Where........................... Date.................

Chittick
Lambertia inermis

Where........................... Date.................

A Coneflower
Isopogon cuneatus

Where........................... Date.................

lls Cranbrook and Gillams Bell are shown. Other nts like the Stirling Range Cone flower. untain Bell and Stirling Range Banksia have eir largest populations here.

Gillams Bell
Darwinia oxylepis

Where........................... Date.................

Cranbrook Bell
Darwinia meeboldii

Where........................... Date.................

tirling Range Banksia
anksia solandri

here........................... Date.................

Mountain Pea
Nemcia leakiana

Where........................... Date.................

Bell Fruited mallee
Eucalyptus preissiana

Where........................... Date.................

Holly-leaved Honeysuckle
Lambertia ilicifolia

Where........................ Date................

Cow Kicks
Stylidium schoenoides

Where......................... Date................

Nematolepis phebalioides

Where.......................... Date................

Mop Bushpea
Urodon dasyphylla

Where...........................Date................

Prickly Poison
Gastrolobium spinosum

Where.......................... Date................

80% of the original native woodland has been cleared in the wheatbelt but there remain a few remnant areas of bush, many thankfully are now gazetted as nature reserves. Dryandra Woodland is one shown above and wherever there exists what we call Kwongan Heath, there can occur incredible densities of wildflowers. Above the beautiful Pink

Ouch Bush
Daviesia pachyphylla

Where........................ Date................

Hakea Obtusa

Where.......................... Date................

Dwarf Burchardia
Burchadia multiflora

Where.......................... Date........

Moss-leaved Heath
Astroloma ciliatum

Where............................ Date.................

Rose Coneflower
Isopogon dubius

Where............................ Date.................

Flat-leaved Wattle
Acacia glaucoptera

Where............................ Date.................

Coneflower *(Isopogon crithmifolius)* and Fine-leaved Smokebush *(Conospermum filfolium subsp filifolium)* can be seen in the foreground. There are numerous reserves that one can visit in the Wheatbelt and if they contain Kwongan heath (sandy soils that are specie rich) like that above, the specie diversity can be breath taking.

Prickly Toothbrush
Grevillea armigera

Where............................ Date.................

Dwarf Grasstree
Xanthorrhoea nana

Where............................ Date.................

Rabbit Orchid
Leptoceras menziesii

Where............................ Date.................

Wax Grevillea
Grevillea insignis subsp. insignis.

Where............................ Date.................

Flame Grevillea
Grevillea excelsior

Where............................ Date.................

Scarlet Pear Gum
Eucalyptus stoatei

Where.......................... Date.................

Leman's Gum
Eucalyptus lehmannii

Where.......................... Date.................

Coral Gum
Eucalyptus torquata

Where.......................... Date.............

Coarse-leaved Mallee
Eucalyptus grossa

Where.......................... Date.................

Four-winged Mallee
Eucalyptus tetraptera

Where.......................... Date.................

Where the land is uncleared or vested in lar
nature reserves, the trees can stretch as far as t
eye can see. There are over 500 recognised spec
and sub specie of Eucalypt in WA. That is a hu
quantity of tree specie. The Eucalypts are a fas
nating genus, botanists identify eucalypts n
necessarily by the flower but more importantly

Gungurru
Eucalyptus caesia subsp caesia

Where.......................... Date.................

Gimlet
Eucalyptus salubris var. salubris

Where.......................... Date.................

Salmon gum
Eucalyptus salmonophloia

Where.......................... Date.................

Green Spider Orchid
Caladenia falcata
Where.......................... Date................

Babe in a cradle *Epiblema grandi-florum subsp grandiflorum*
Where.......................... Date................

Custard Orchid
Thelymitra villosa
Where.......................... Date................

the flower buds, fruit, leaves and bark.
under the eucalypt canopy many orchids find their
home again Western Australia is blessed with a
massive selection of orchid specie there being
several hundred. The largest group that occur in
Western Australia are the terrestrial (ground
living) orchids just a few being shown on this page.

Christmas leek Orchid
Prasophyllum brownii
Where.......................... Date................

Common Donkey Orchid
Diurus corymbosa
Where.......................... Date................

ug Orchid
terostylis recurva
here.......................... Date................

Queen of Sheba Orchid
Thelymitra variegata
Where.......................... Date................

Red Beaks
Burnettia nigricans
Where.......................... Date................

WILDFLOWERS NORTH OF PERTH

Common lamb Poison
Isotropis cuneifolia

Where.......................... Date................

Holly Pea
Jacksonia floribunda

Where.......................... Date................

Coppercups
Pileanthus peduncularis

Where.......................... Date................

Rusty Lambstails
Lachnostachys ferruginea

Where.......................... Date................

Ashby's Banksia
Banksia ashbyi

Where.......................... Date................

In late spring to early summer just north of Perth particularly in Moore River National Park off the Brand Highway masses of bright yellow Morrison Featherflowers *(Verticordia nitens)* cover the landscape while above the lemon yellow mass flowe

Velvet Fanflower
Scaevola phlebopetala

Where.......................... Date................

Honey Bush
Hakea lissocarpha

Where.......................... Date................

Button Creeper
Tersonia cyathiflora

Where.......................... Date................

taghorn Bush
aviesia epiphylla

here............................ Date.................

Yellow Lechenaultia
Lechenaultia linarioides

Where............................ Date.................

Violet Eremaea
Eremaea violacea

Where............................ Date.................

eads of the Slender Banksia *(Banksia attenuata)* edominate. Another very restricted Banksia the opeller Banksia *(Banksia candolleana)* can be seen re as well as Winter Bells *(Blancoa canescens)* but ey are more prolific in early spring.

Pearl Flower
Conostephium pendulum

Where............................ Date.................

Many-flowered Honeysuckle
Lambertia multiflora redform

Where............................ Date.................

inter Bell
lancoa canescens

here............................ Date.................

Red Swamp Cranberry
Astroloma stmarrhena

Where............................ Date.................

Propeller Banksia
Banksia candolleana

Where............................ Date.................

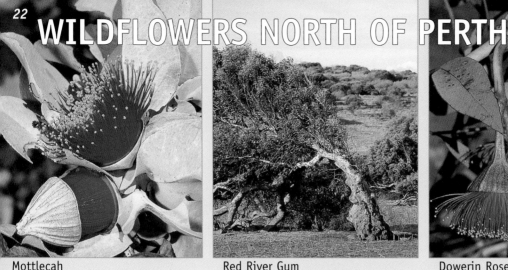

Mottlecah
Eucalyptus macrocarpa

Where........................... Date.................

Red River Gum
Eucalyptus camaldulensis

Where........................... Date.................

Dowerin Rose
Eucalyptus pyriformis red form

Where........................... Date.............

Illyarrie
Eucalyptus erythrocorys

Where........................... Date.................

Scarlet Featherflower
Verticordia grandis

Where........................... Date.................

Travelling further north on the Brand Highway th
areas around Badgingarra and Eneabba contain son
of the highest densities of wildflowers anywhere
Australia. We call this region the Northern Sandpla
much of it being sandy Kwongan heath with litera
hundreds of specie in just a 100 metre square bloc

Common Catspaw
Anigozanthus humilis subsp. humilis

Where........................... Date.................

Acorn Banksia
Banksia prionotes

Where........................... Date.................

Ribbed Hakea
Hakea costata

Where........................... Date..........

Shell-leaved Hakea
Hakea conchifolia

Where............................ Date.................

Pink Pockers
Grevillea petrophiloides

Where............................ Date.................

23

Needle Tree
Hakea preissii

Where............................ Date.................

Here alongside the highway north of Badgingarra, masses of Yellow Kangaroo Paw *(Anigozanthos pulcherrimus)* cover the sandplain with the bright pink flowers of Summer Coppercups *(Pileanthus filiolius)* adding colour in the foreground contrasting with the white smokebush *(Conosperum sp)*.

Sceptre Banksia
Banksia sceptrum

Where............................ Date.................

Shaggy Dryandra
Dryandra speciosa

Where............................ Date.................

Black Kangaroo Paw
Macropida fuliginosa

Where............................ Date.................

Geraldton Wax
Chamelaucium uncinatum

Where............................ Date.................

Wreath Lechenaultia
Lechenaultia macrantha

Where............................ Date.................

WILDFLOWERS NORTH OF PERTH

Red Pokers
Hakea bucculenta

Where.......................... Date................

Cricket Ball hakea
Hakea platysperma

Where.......................... Date................

Emu Tree
Hakea francisiana

Where.......................... Date............

Fan Hakea
Hakea baxteri

Where.......................... Date................

Curly Grevillea
Grevillea erynigiodes

Where.......................... Date................

The Kalbarri National Park illustrated above aga contains a huge variety of wildflowers, here there a wildflowers blooming all year such is the richness this region. In late spring early summer Pir Cauliflower *(Verticordia monadelpha var. callittricha*

Blue Tinsel Lily
Calectasia grandiflora

Where.......................... Date................

Keraudrenia integrifolia

Where.......................... Date................

Pixie Mops
Petrophile linearis

Where.......................... Date............

White-plumed Grevillea
Grevillea leucopteris

Where............................ Date.................

Blue-eyed Smokebush
Conospermum brownii

Where............................ Date.................

Painted Featherflower
Verticordia picta

Where............................ Date.................

White Plumed Grevilleas (*Grevillea leucopteris*) and Sceptre Banksia (*Banksia sceptrum*) line the side of the road leading to the Kalbarri townsite in late spring early summer. Earlier the rapier like stems of Acacia latipes are in full bloom.

Common Cauliflower
Verticordia eriocephala

Where............................ Date.................

Pink Cauliflower
Verticordia monadelpha var. callitricha

Where............................ Date.................

Acacia latipes

Where............................ Date.................

Oldfields Foxglove
Pityrodia oldfiedii

Where............................ Date.................

Woolly Featherflowers *Verticordia monodelpha var. monadelpha, white form*

Where............................ Date.................

Jam
Acacia accuminata

Where.......................... Date................

Bottlebrush Grevillea
Grevillea paradoxa

Where.......................... Date................

Tall Mulla Mulla
Ptilotus exaltatus

Where.......................... Date.............

Native Cornflower
Brunonia australis

Where.......................... Date................

Bright Podolepis
Podolepis canescens

Where.......................... Date................

Driving north or north east the traveller leaves t
outer Wheatbelt then passes through the transitio
al eucalypt woodland and enters a type of habitat w
call the 'Mulga'. Some of this country stretches f
hundreds miles and it is easy to get lost in, so
very careful. This region is one of the strongholds
the group of flowers called 'everlasting
Predominately from the daisy group. If winter rai

Fragrant Waitzia
Waitzia suaveolens

Where.......................... Date................

Native Daisy
Brachyscome iberidifolia

Where.......................... Date................

Featherheads
Ptilotus macrocephalus

Where.......................... Date..........

lannel Bush
olanum lasiophyllum

here............................ Date..................

Tar Bush
Eremophila glabra

Where............................ Date.................

Turpentine Bush
Eremophila fraseri

Where............................ Date.................

Sandlewood
Santalum spicatum

Where............................ Date.................

ave been prolific, then the Mulga understorey can
e covered as far as the eye can see with everlasting
aisies. Sometimes there can be a dense concentra-
on of everlasting specie such as above. Here in the
reground Tall Mulla Mulla *(Ptilotus exaltatus)* and
een Pussytail's *(Ptilotus macrocephalus)* flourish
hile in the background dense bushes of Silver Tails
Ptilotus obovatus) grow.

A Poverty Bush
Eremophila foliosissima

Where............................ Date.................

turt's Desert Pea
wainsona formosa

here............................ Date..................

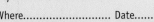

Upside down Pea
Leptosema daviesiodes

Where............................ Date.................

Wilcox Bush
Eremophila forrestii

Where............................ Date............

WILDFLOWERS NORTH OF PERTH

Darwin Woolybutt
Eucalyptus miniata

Where......................... Date................

Kimberley heath
Calytrix existipulata

Where........................... Date.................

Blue Grevillea
Grevillea agrifolia

Where........................... Date.............

Purnululu Palm
Livistonea victoriai

Where......................... Date................

The Kimberley would have to be one the author's favourite destinations, here in the rugged north is region that has been cut off from the south part of the State by the vast Great Sandy Desert. The Boa perhaps typifies the Kimberley and the many gorges hold water throughout the year. This was a land whe the indigenous peoples never were short of bush tucker. Water lilly roots; certain flowers buds and the see of the Spinifex were all used as natural foods.

Sticky Kurrajong
Sterculia visciddula

Where......................... Date.................

Yellow Kapok
Cochlospermum fraseri

Where........................... Date.................

Boab
Adansonia gregorii

Where........................... Date..........